From Frazzled
to Fabulous

From **Frazzled** *to* **Fabulous**

How to juggle a successful career,
fatherhood, 'me-time'
and looking good

from
**The Man Who
Has It All**

BANTAM PRESS

LONDON · NEW YORK · TORONTO · SYDNEY · AUCKLAND

TRANSWORLD PUBLISHERS
61–63 Uxbridge Road, London W5 5SA
www.penguin.co.uk

Transworld is part of the Penguin Random House group of companies
whose addresses can be found at global.penguinrandomhouse.com

Penguin
Random House
UK

First published in Great Britain in 2016 by Bantam Press
an imprint of Transworld Publishers

A CIP catalogue record for this book
is available from the British Library.

ISBN 9780593077863

Typeset in Avenir Next Regular 11/15pt by Falcon Oast Graphic Art Ltd.
Printed and bound by Printer Trento, Italy.

Penguin Random House is committed to a sustainable
future for our business, our readers and our planet. This book
is made from Forest Stewardship Council® certified paper.

MIX
Paper from
responsible sources
FSC® C018179

1 3 5 7 9 10 8 6 4 2

Acknowledgements

I'm grateful to all my supporters on Twitter and Facebook and to the busy dads who found the time to help me with research for this book. I am grateful to my agent and editor who have put up with my hormonal fluctuations and tendency to overreact. And of course I am grateful to my wife for letting me have a little project of my own.

Contents

Foreword

IN THE EARLY HOURS **of 31 October 2015, I tripped over the cat's water bowl, stubbed my toe and knocked a bag of icing sugar on to my wife's open laptop. I wasn't looking where I was going due to exhaustion and lack of sleep. It was 1.40 a.m. My Halloween cupcakes were still in the oven and from the floor above I could hear my six-year-old son shouting, 'Daddy!' from his bedroom.**

In the moments that followed I felt resentful, guilty and sad. I resented my wife for being asleep – seemingly oblivious to our nocturnal son and my frantic cake decorating. I felt guilty about my poor organizational skills. What kind of dad leaves his baking until the night before? I felt sad for my son, who didn't always have the happy, joyful daddy he deserved.

In the wake of my trip, I asked myself some tough questions. Was this really the life I wanted? Did I want to be a stressed-out, manic husband and dad? And, more importantly, what was I going to do with my wife's laptop? In desperation, I dabbed at the keyboard with a damp cloth, pushing the sugar between the keys and icing them together.

As I closed the lid of my wife's sticky laptop and switched off the lights, I heard the welcome sound of silence and realized my son must have gone back to sleep. I'll be honest with you, I'd completely forgotten about him. The pain, the cakes, the laptop . . . This was the wake-up call I needed. If I couldn't be there for my child in the night, what kind of dad was I?

As I hobbled back to bed, I caught sight of my face in the mirror. My hair was greasy, my complexion was dull and my eyes were puffy. I just didn't look like me. Where had the old me gone? Was he still in there? It was at this moment I realized I had a choice. I could carry on as I was – guilty, stressed and exhausted. Or I could get a grip and radically change my life.

Looking back, I should have made the change sooner. But this book isn't about beating myself up. It's about celebrating what I have become and sharing it with you. I have finally found that elusive balance between work and family. I have three healthy kids, a beautiful home, a successful wife and my own career. I even have time to decorate my cupcakes!

Whilst I don't pretend to have all the answers, I nudge men to rediscover their confidence and gain control over their lives. In these pages I take men by the hand and gently draw them away from the pressure of perfection to become what we all want to be – a man who has it all.

@manwhohasitall, 2016

1

Choosing to Thrive

Fathers in the Workplace

NEARLY HALF OF ALL **managers admit to thinking twice when it comes to hiring men who have children. But the experience of raising a child can actually make men well suited to the workplace. Companies who do not hire fathers could be turning down an extremely valuable resource.**

In this chapter, I bust the myths surrounding fathers in the workplace and call for a more flexible, open and compassionate approach from managers.

Every man has different reasons for his choices and I respect that. This chapter is about those men who, for whatever reason, choose to work.

Doubt

Leaving your kids to go out to work is tough. But, believe it or not, dads do survive. In fact, research shows that children of a career dad can do just as well as children of a stay-at-home dad. Working dads can absolutely be great parents; it's all about achieving that elusive balance.

Every working dad has a different reason for going to work. We should support each other's choices, even if they are wrong.

TALKING POINT

Being ignored, mistaken for the tea gentleman or branded a 'paternity risk'. Are men overreacting when it comes to issues they face at work?

Identity

Being a working dad can boost your self-esteem and give you an identity beyond just 'Dad'. When you have kids, you put yourself at the bottom of the heap. Working reminds you that you are a person in your own right. Fathers are often grateful for the opportunity to be around other adults and reclaim their former child-free selves.

Dad skills

Because children require so much attention, fathers are super-organized and multitasking aces. Don't minimize the skills you learn as a dad. Here are some of the things I have learned:

- Organizational skills
- Persistence
- Flexibility
- Saying 'no'
- Patience
- Empathy
- Gratitude

TIP

To all independent men. Don't be **afraid** of your independence! It's OK to be a man and be independent. Some women **actually** find it attractive.

Flexible working

Before you consider embarking on any kind of paid work, remember to ask about family-friendly perks. Some companies make very generous allowances for fathers in the workplace. You shouldn't be afraid to take advantage of them!

TALKING POINT
Are men in the workplace a **distraction?**

But flexibility can mean different things to different men. It could mean working for one day, or even one hour per week, whatever you feel you can manage.

REAL-LIFE DADS

'*Everyone* I work with knows that I am a dad. I don't try to hide it and pretend to be focused only on my work.'

Dean, 39

Becoming a valued team member

Making friends and being liked is important for getting ahead at work. But being likeable isn't the only measure of success. Don't forget that there are other ways to gain respect. For example, you could offer to organize the Christmas party, look after cards and gifts for leavers, keep the staff kitchen clean, run the tea kitty or offer to wash tea towels at the weekend. Your watchwords are 'helpful', 'polite' and 'nice'. If you can achieve just one of these, you will become a valuable member of your team.

> **FACT**
> (i) Many employers value fathers in the workplace because they work on average **three times harder** than their **child-free** counterparts.

Dadpreneurs

For dads who feel daunted by the prospect of fitting in a full-time job alongside everything else, there are many ways to earn a bit of pocket money on the side. Why not join the growing band of 'dadpreneurs'? Earning your own money means you won't feel guilty when you splash out on that new pair of little black trousers! Here are a few money-making ideas to bring out your inner entrepreneur:

- ✳ Babysitting
- ✳ Flower arranging
- ✳ Selling unwanted items on eBay
- ✳ Dog sitting
- ✳ Card making
- ✳ Underpants parties
- ✳ Pampering parties
- ✳ Daddy blogging

TALKING POINT

Should men who are planning to start a family be **legally obliged** to tell their employer?

If you were a high-flying career man in your previous life, try not to worry about taking a break. After all, who doesn't want to be his own boss? This could be your chance to do what you've always wanted to do – and this time it's for you. You could even hook up with like-minded business-savvy dads and join a network such as 'Dads in Business' or 'Men in the Enterprise Hub'. These little get-togethers are not all tea and cake.

Having an Opinion

WHEN EXPRESSING AN OPINION, **some men find it hard to come across as measured and informed. Opinionated men often alienate others by being bossy and outspoken, giving all men a bad name. When you're a man with a fierce opinion, ironically, people will have a lot of opinions about you. Don't let this stop you from piping up. You have every right to express your opinion in whatever way you choose. I offer men tips on how to be opinionated with grace and good humour.**

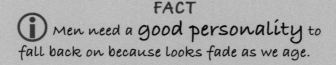

FACT
Men need a good personality to fall back on because looks fade as we age.

Developing confidence

It is not only attractive but actually very healthy for a man to have an opinion of his own. If you're unsure of yourself, listen to your wife's opinions to get one or two ideas. Eventually, as you gain confidence, you may develop your own voice.

If you struggle to make your voice heard at work, try making yourself more visible. Researchers found that men who physically lean in at professional meetings are less likely to be interrupted. Men who lean away, shrinking into themselves, are harder to see and therefore find it harder to be heard.

Pitfalls

Beware, however, of becoming strident, deep-voiced or loud. Regardless of what they say, people don't like opinionated men. It is absolutely fine to express a view if asked, but take care not to overdo it.

Opinionated men often appear awkward or disagreeable. This can be a real turn-off. A man with an opinion should remain calm, agree with others and always be mindful of how he's coming across. If in doubt, remain silent. Whatever the rights and wrongs of it, many

---

TIP

✔ Do people accuse you of being 'difficult and awkward' for expressing an opinion? Maybe you could turn the dial down? Just a little.

---

women prefer their man to say very little or nothing at all. Men should only be professionally and publicly opinionated on the topics of hair, clothes, baking or childcare. This may not seem fair because no one ever questions a woman with an opinion. But smart men know that life isn't fair; they just get on with it.

Why women interrupt men

We speak up in a meeting, only to hear a woman's voice pitch in louder. We put forward an idea, perhaps too uncertainly, only to have a woman repeat it with authority. We may possess the skill, but she has the right vocal cords – which means we shut up, losing our confidence (or, worse, the credit for the work). The reason for this is not – as it seems to many men – that women seek to deny men a voice. It is simply a matter of style. Women are naturally better at dominating the conversation than they are at taking turns. Equally, men are better listeners, preferring to nurture relationships and make connections. So next time a woman interrupts you, be patient: she can't help it.

TALKING POINT

How important is it for a man to be **adorable** when expressing an opinion?

The dos and don'ts of having an opinion

DO	DON'T
Be agreeable	Be difficult
Be sassy	Be ungentlemanlike
Be nice	Speak ill of other men
Lift other men up	Be selfish
Listen	Speak over other men
Remain rational	Get too emotional
Shut up	Raise your voice

REAL MEN

'My girlfriend says I look **cute** when I'm feisty.'

Henry, 28

> **TIP**
> ✔ Are you viewed as 'challenging and loud' for talking in a normal voice at work? Why not try whispering instead?

Don't be aggressive, be assertive

You're in a board meeting and the woman sitting opposite you slams her fist down on the table as she makes her point. Another woman gets to her feet to shout her disagreement from across the room. No one bats an eyelid. These two are clearly passionate businesswomen. You speak up, with just as much enthusiasm, only to be told there's no need to be aggressive. Being assertive is all about adopting a respectful tone and minimizing your threat level to zero. There is a fine line between being aggressive and being assertive. Master it by practising a few simple skills:

* Don't make statements, ask questions
* Admit that you're not 100 per cent sure
* Ask a woman what she thinks
* Smile and laugh

> **TIP**
> ✔ Use skincare products with the 'glow factor' if you want to be seen and heard at the boardroom table.

The opinionated man

The phrase 'an opinionated man' carries a special sting. It is a code phrase for 'outspoken' and 'threatening'. Your words, no matter how well chosen, will be heard through the filter of being a man: hormone-crazed. The phrase suggests that having XY chromosomes and opinions is unmanly. If a woman calls you not just 'opinionated' but 'an opinionated man', beware: she may be trying to shut you down.

> **FACT**
> ⓘ Behind every strong, sexy, opinionated man is a woman who loves him just the way he is.

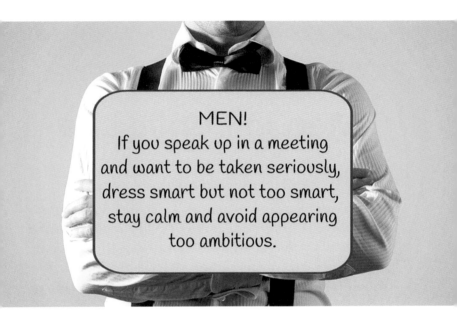

MEN!
If you speak up in a meeting
and want to be taken seriously,
dress smart but not too smart,
stay calm and avoid appearing
too ambitious.

Having an opinion in public

An opinionated man can be a huge embarrassment to his wife in social situations. We all know what it feels like to be in the company of Little Mr Chatterbox – the man who just doesn't know when to shut up. For this reason, I always advise men to be informed as well as opinionated. Being informed means having know-ledge about the subject. If you're not prepared to do your homework, don't expect people to listen to what you have to say. It's simply a matter of respect.

Men in Public Life

FROM MALE EXPERTS ON **panels to male magistrates, there are exceptional men in every area of public life. So many amazing men work hard to represent other men and ensure their voices are heard. We shouldn't be afraid to celebrate these men and make their achievements visible. In this section, in the hope of inspiring others, I highlight the journeys just a few of these incredible men have made towards success.**

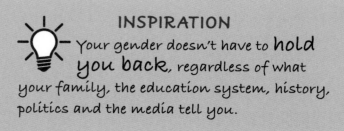

INSPIRATION
Your gender doesn't have to **hold you back**, regardless of what your family, the education system, history, politics and the media tell you.

I believe there should be at least one man at every boardroom table in business, within the highest echelons of the Civil Service, in the top ranks of our political parties and in every area of public life. Men have proven themselves to be competent committee members, secretaries and chairwomen. It is true that women are neutral and are able to represent everyone, but men do have real-life experiences to offer. If men's voices aren't heard, an important part of the debate is overlooked. Let's welcome more of them to the corridors of power.

There are two barriers to recruiting more men to board positions. The first barrier is inner confidence and the second is other men.

Confidence

There are few things more handsome in a man than confidence. Men who wear it radiate enthusiasm, passion and positivity. Confidence contributes more to a man's look than an expensive watch or haircut. When a man knows who he is, he is absolutely gorgeous.

ALLIES

'I genuinely don't have a problem with men in public life, as long as they are able to represent everyone, and not just **men** and **men's issues**.'

Samantha,
non-executive director

A confident man is not afraid to be himself. Whether he is plain and mousy or feisty and fabulous, the key is that he knows who he is. He understands his purpose and his gifts. A confident man dresses with style. It doesn't matter whether he prefers a casual shirt, jeans and trainers, or a smart shirt, trousers and shoes. What is most important is that he is himself.

Unfortunately, most men struggle with confidence issues. Whilst women are born with confidence, men have to search for it deep within themselves. Some men describe their confidence as a pip or a seed; others say it's more of a feeling or an aura. Finding your inner confidence is a journey – often a long one, with many ups and downs along the way. Some men find their confidence early in life, only to lose it again. Others never find it. Some don't even know where to look.

ALLIES

'I have nothing **against** male representatives on conference panels, as long as they don't take up the place of an expert.'

Shalini, CEO

For men, confidence is the ability to:

✳ Speak up in a meeting.

✳ Hold your head up high, whether you are fat, thin or somewhere in between.

✳ Walk into a room full of people, even though your skin might be less than perfect.

✳ Trust that a smile and a pleasant manner will be what interests and engages others.

ALLIES

'I have absolutely **nothing** against male newspaper editors, as long as they don't fill the paper with stories about men and men's issues.'

Pearl, editor

'I'm not hung up on the label "chairwoman" because I know it covers both women and men.'

Liam, 31, chairwoman

TALKING POINT

Should 25 per cent of boardroom positions be held by men? Or is that too high, as so many women suggest?

Support

The biggest barrier to our success is, of course, each other. Men, I hate to say it, but the stereotype is true: we are our own worst enemies. Men can be so mean. Instead of lifting each other up, we tear each other down. We disagree on matters of childcare, house-keeping, work and even politics. Imagine how much we could achieve if we supported one another. Indeed, we should create our own men's networks and clubs. What can *you* do to support another man in public life?

ALLIES

'No, I don't think **all** men are stupid. I've met some **very** bright ones in my time. I would have no hesitation inviting one to interview.'

Sophia, CEO

Alan, husband, dad of three, mentor and dadpreneur, 53

Alan has his own Etsy business selling gorgeous homemade crafts. He sits on the Men in Enterprise board and mentors other budding dadpreneurs.

During his working life, Alan has experienced some challenges, in particular regarding how some people perceive opinionated, ambitious men. Alan overcame these barriers by improving his posture and getting an inspirational male mentor.

Alan's advice to other men is: *'Always challenge your comfort zone, support other wonderful men and keep your energy levels up by snacking on dried fruit during the day. Be confident in your own abilities and don't be afraid to talk in a normal speaking voice if you have something to say.'*

Quotas

The issue of quotas divides people. Radical men argue that males should be entitled to a certain number of senior positions in all areas of public life. Some go as far as to suggest that 30 per cent of senior positions in organizations should be occupied by men. Others believe that men should be promoted on the basis of merit alone, rather than based purely on their gender.

I believe that quotas go a step too far. If we want more men in positions of authority, we should be prepared to work hard for that privilege and not be handed it on a plate to fill a quota. Some men moan about 'intractable barriers' and the 'glass ceiling', as if they have swallowed a dictionary. My message is this: stop coming up with excuses and just get on with it. If dadpreneurs like Alan can do it, so can you.

Male Politicians

I T IS IMPORTANT THAT every area of public life benefits from men's contributions, but it is especially important in politics. For this reason, 'Men in Politics' deserves its own chapter. Men make a significant contribution to running the country, and we should celebrate this.

We can be particularly proud of our male politicians. Men bring so much more than just their good looks, style and *je ne sais quoi* to the table. However, we must remember that men are not all the same and they do not speak with one voice.

The following pages pose some important questions about men's issues, men's role in politics and male representation.

The problem

For there to be more men in politics, males must have the confidence to stand for election. We can hardly blame political parties for not putting male candidates forward if there simply aren't any. Some people argue that men can't hack the cut and thrust

of politics. Being an MP *is* a demanding job, not for the faint-hearted. But evidence suggests that with the right posture, flexible working options and style advice, men make very good politicians.

So what really holds men back? Many theories have been put forward – the lack of childcare, the old girls' club mentality and the difficulty in finding a male toilet in Parliament. However, this doesn't explain why some men make it to the top and others don't. What can we learn from those who succeed?

TIP

✔ To get ahead in politics, seek advice from an image consultant to avoid coming across as frumpy or, worse, overly sexual.

Caution

Some male politicians go too far the other way, rejecting the very masculinity that they should be celebrating, thus giving all men a bad name. I overheard a particularly strident male MP say, 'I don't like being called a "male politician". I'm just a politician.' Personally, I don't see any need for this. After all, he *is* a male politician!

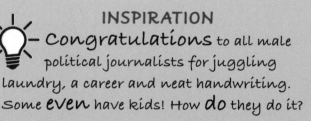

INSPIRATION
Congratulations to all male political journalists for juggling laundry, a career and neat handwriting. Some *even* have kids! How *do* they do it?

There is evidence to suggest that male MPs bring different issues to the table. According to several studies, the presence of males in politics influences domestic policy and can even have an indirect impact on spending priorities. However, it does not necessarily follow that male MPs serve the interests of men as a whole.

ALLIES

'Congratulations to all male cabinet ministers for getting there on merit alone. Very well done, all of you.'

Patricia, Minister for Men

Male representation

A lot of importance is attached to the idea of achieving 'male representation'. However, once we start saying we need men in Parliament, it follows that we need to have every group represented. The whole principle opens up a Pandora's box. Whatever next? Children in the Welsh Assembly? Bunny rabbits in Parliament?

ALLIES

'I'm all for male politicians. They bring a **unique** perspective. And, if I'm allowed to say this, they **brighten** the place up!'

— Kate, MP

The theory is that if people can see male MPs in a political party, that party is likely to represent the interests of men as a whole. However, when people were asked whether they wanted their MP to have a particular characteristic, researchers were surprised to find that being a male came at the bottom of the list for both women and men.

DID YOU KNOW?

Men already have many of the necessary skills for politics; for example, the ability to cooperate, listening skills, social skills and **empathy**.

Men and Humour

WHO SAYS MEN CAN'T **be funny? I reject the common myth that men are humourless and can't take a joke. It's simply not true. We can laugh at ourselves and laugh at each other. Here, I offer some tips on how to use humour to your advantage. I end with advice on how to deal with jokes that make you feel uncomfortable.**

TALKING POINT

Is it **really** true that men don't need to have a sense of humour because they can attract women by **looking nice**?

Despite what you might think, funny men aren't always a turn-off. Some women actually find a man with a sense of humour attractive. Just remember to laugh at her jokes too! Every woman likes to think she is funny. Don't bruise her fragile female ego! It's your job to laugh at her jokes as well as try out a few of your own.

If you don't understand a joke immediately, try not to worry about it. Ask whoever is telling the joke to explain it to you slowly. It's a generalization that men can't take a joke – we just need to give ourselves permission to laugh. To avoid coming across as uptight, take time out to nurture your sense of humour.

Male comedy

Despite the proliferation of funny men in the main-stream, audiences have to acclimatize to the astringent sassiness of male humour. For that reason, stand-up comedy can be an uncomfortable place for men. We are so often the butt of the joke – stereotyped as fathers-in-law, nagging husbands or sex objects. If you don't like this sort of humour, don't go and see it. Most men get the joke and find it hilarious. So instead of criticizing it, ask yourself why you're the only one not laughing.

REAL MEN

'The **really** shocking thing is, even though I'm a man myself, there are some male comedians I **just don't find funny**. Am I allowed to say that?'

Steve, 50

REAL MEN

'My wife thinks men **can** be funny. She thinks I'm a funny little thing and she's probably right! I'm so lucky.'

Bryan, 40

Many men call themselves comedians and have their own shows. I applaud this. The stage is still seen by some women as not a natural place for a man to be. Even young, slim, attractive male comedians struggle with confidence and self-belief. Keeping your composure when someone is shouting at you to get your penis out isn't easy, but if you're not happy to get your penis out on stage, perhaps you're not cut out for stand-up. Men who struggle to cope with the pressure often return to being full-time dads.

My advice to any man considering a career in comedy is to think very carefully about how they will appear to women. Do you want to put yourself in the spotlight? Is there really a market for it? Regardless, I have absolutely no problem with male comedians, as long as they are funny.

Some women like to wind men up by telling deliberately cruel jokes. For example, a hilarious woman I know called Claire told one of her team, Liam, this joke: 'I think men are really equal. Equally good at making me a sandwich!'

Liam didn't understand the joke and didn't laugh.

DID YOU KNOW?
Laughing burns 58 **calories** a minute.

Banter

Banter is a verb and a noun describing the playful and friendly exchange of teasing remarks. Most people love it. People banter at work, in the pub and at family gatherings. Banter is either something you have or you don't. There is no middle ground when it comes to banter. Some men argue that banter is a cloak used by women to legitimize teasing and bullying. Unfortunately, these humourless men open themselves up to even more banter. What would be your retort to Claire who asked Liam to make her a sandwich?

Communication Skills

I N THIS SECTION, I urge men to think about how they communicate at work and in relationships. Sometimes we forget the power of simply being silent when communicating with others. Men are often criticized for the pitch, tone and volume of their voices. (Have *you* ever been accused of shouting when you thought you were talking normally?) For this reason, men should pay as much attention to the way they come across as they do to their diet, clothes and skincare regime. I offer tips and tricks on how to appear assertive, calm and unflappable in all communications.

The male brain

In the area of the brain that controls empathy and listening, men have 43.2 per cent more neurons than women. The principal centre for emotion, called the heppiclomptus, controls a whopping 57.1 per cent of the male brain. This gives the male brain fabulous and unique qualities, such as emotional intelligence, the ability to multitask effortlessly, male instinct, an almost psychic ability to read facial expressions and the desire to nurture others. All of this is hardwired into the brains of men, whether they like it or not. Science tells us that men are born with these amazing qualities. Women are born with other talents, for example, logic, reasoning, rationality and leadership skills.

ALLIES

'I **love** bossy men. I could be around them all day. To me, bossy is not a bad thing. It means somebody is strong and isn't **afraid** to take control.'

Reena, engineer

Communication styles

FEMALE COMMUNICATION STYLES	MALE COMMUNICATION STYLES
Straight to the point	Tendency to talk around the subject
Clear and direct	All over the place
Logical	Emotional
Authoritative	Agreeable and a bit vague
Ability to see the bigger picture	Ability to remember insignificant details

Communication in relationships

Men have an incredible innate ability to remember birthdays, anniversaries and the names of friends' partners and children. Women are simply not able to remember these details because of differences in how their brains store information.

Men can be overemotional in relationships and overreact about the smallest things. Women take a more measured, reasonable and objective approach to conflict. Understanding these natural differences can prevent tensions from arising in the first place.

INSPIRATION

Don't think that your contribution isn't worthwhile because of your gender. You can be a man and **still** make a very valid point.

TALKING POINT

Should women try to include men in meetings by asking **them** what they think? Or is it up to men to speak more clearly?

Women and men enjoy doing different things in their spare time. Men enjoy cleaning, shopping, ironing, sorting through all the kids' clothes that no longer fit and gossiping. Women, on the other hand, enjoy physical challenges and intellectual pursuits, with a clear-headed focus on achievement and personal mastery. Women and men are equal, but different. Playing to your strengths is the key to success in any relationship.

Communication at work

Professional men often experience significant challenges in communicating powerfully with gravitas and authority. Science tells us that there is a reason for this.

Much of men's weakness at work is influenced by their hormones and brain chemistry. These natural chemicals interfere with the part of the brain that controls intellect and language.

TALKING POINT
Do men talk too much? Or is it just a few **bad apples** giving us all a bad name?

Instead of focusing on the task in hand, men tend to overthink things and experience them with deep emotionality. This needn't hold men back. In fact, many of the most successful men use their emotional intelligence to their advantage. Men make the most wonderful primary-school teachers, counsellors, carers and social workers. Emotional intelligence can also be a real plus when working on a checkout or taking care of little ones.

Six communication sins:

✸ Talking too much

✸ Not talking enough

✸ Raising your voice at the beginning, middle or end of a sentence

✸ Interrupting when a woman is speaking

✸ Having a male voice

✸ Existing as a man

MEN! Don't hide your intelligence. It's OK to be a man and have a brain. Some women actually find it attractive.

REAL MEN

Do women explain things to you?
Simply because you're a man?
'Yes, and I really appreciate it.'

Rob, 45

A note on bossy men

The stereotypical career man is bossy, selfish, icy and unsympathetic. He is like a strict headmaster telling everyone what to do. But is the stereotype true? I interviewed a number of career men whilst research- ing this book and I found them all competent, professional and lovely. Men can be strong leaders without being Mr Bossy Pants. Instead of shouting and finger-wagging, you should try to exert your authority with your body language. A man can get things done with his warmth, passion and empathy.

Bossy boys grow up to be bossy men. They go from bossing other little boys around to bossing other men around. If you have always been a bossy little mister, turn this into a positive.

Confidence in the workplace

I asked busy life coach Andrew to share his top tips for men who struggle with confidence in the workplace.

Andrew, Life Coach

'The tone of voice a man uses can make or break his success at work. If it's too deep, he should enlist the help of a voice coach.

'A colour pop can give any working man a lift. He should choose a bold colour near his face and choose one or two bright accessories to give his outfit personality.'

Q&A

Question: 'I don't like the fact that women always speak over me in meetings. What should I do?'

Answer: 'Just don't say anything. No one is making you.'

'f it were up to me, I'd have at :ast one man at every boardroom ible. I love men. They are such icinating creatures.'

Sally, CEO

2

That Elusive
Balance

Career or Baby?

PICK UP ANY MEN'S **magazine and you will find a debate on the right time to start a family. Many experts advise men to have babies earlier, while others insist it's better to have your career first and then start a family.**

It's all about what is right for you.

However, all men should have the chance to have a family and a career. Society must do more to enable fathers to play a full and active role, not only at home, but in the workplace too.

Men: is there ever a right time to have a baby?

So when is best for a man to have a baby? Statistics show that we're leaving it later, sometimes to our cost. More men are choosing to delay fatherhood until their late thirties and forties. It is difficult for men because life expectancy is increasing, so a forty-five-year-old doesn't feel his age. But his testicles tell a different story.

DID YOU KNOW?

Most men become broody as they hit their twenties and **desperate** for a baby as they hit their thirties. This is a hardwired, biological response designed to continue the species. It is nothing to be **afraid** of.

Tick tock

There's no getting away from the biological reality. 'The aim should be to start a family before thirty-eight, certainly by forty,' says Dr Karen Smith of the Birmingham Men's Fertility Centre. 'It becomes much harder after the age of forty-five. Older men have fewer and slower-swimming sperm.'

REAL-LIFE DADS

'I **struggled** to combine raising children with having a high-powered job. I found that eating just **six almonds** a day gave me the energy I needed to tackle both.'

Mark, 45

So that's the bad news. Now for the good news. There is plenty a man can do to maintain his fertility for longer. Getting up earlier could improve fertility too. Before trying to become a dad, it may be worth having a cucumber detox at your local spa.

Child-free men

If a man approaches forty and still doesn't have kids, he will find himself defending his decision, even if he's single. People question whether a child-free man can ever truly be happy. Society often refers to men without children as bachelors and paints an

Are child-free men selfish?

unfavourable picture of them, living alone with a house full of dogs and scented candles. This is totally unfair and does not represent childless men. Some childless men actually live full and meaningful lives.

Celebrating difference

I fully support all men's choices – men who have kids, career men and men who have it all. We must stop defining men by fertility and fatherhood. Men have so much more to offer than this. When I talk to men who say they 'have it all,' their advice to other dads is always: 'Do what is right for you.' I never evangelize about my own decisions in life, even though I would advise any man to make the same choices I have. Instead, I insist on every man's right to choose what is best for him.

Getting Organized

A GOOD DAD IS A **well-organized dad. Here I give away the secrets of a successful home – using a family planner, keeping the freezer well stocked and preparing everything the night before. I draw on interviews with other super-dads as well as my own experience. Do you have a daddy friend who is super-productive? Do you marvel at how much stuff he gets done in a day? Have you ever wanted to know how on earth he does it? I give busy dads advice on how to take the manic out of manic mornings. Simple, easy and practical tips can shave seconds if not minutes off the morning routine, giving Dad more 'me-time'.**

Family planners

A family planner is an essential tool for the busiest person of them all – Dad! Navigate fatherhood with a wall planner, ring binder or just a simple A4 pad. Whatever works for your family. Keep a list of numbers for the babysitter, school, plumber, children's friends' parents, piano teacher, dentist, etc. You can also use it

REAL-LIFE DADS

How do you raise kids and have a career in tech at the same time?

'I get **everything** ready the night before.'

Hamish, 30

to keep track of everyone's movements by giving your wife and kids their own special sections. Use helpful sticky notes and colourful pens to keep them interested – you could even motivate them with gold stars. When life gets crazy, your family planner is in control.

REAL-LIFE DADS

'I have always struggled getting everything done. My **Organized Dad Weekly Household Planner** breaks tasks into easy manageable chunks. This keeps me sane and prevents me from being **totally** overwhelmed!'

Edward, 32

Make-ahead meals

Let's face it, we all buy ready meals and takeaways occasionally. It's so much easier when you've had a manic day. You're a busy dad – we know that. But that doesn't mean your family's health should suffer!

REAL-LIFE DADS
'I'd be a **complete** mess if I didn't have a well-stocked freezer.'

Omar, 30

Cooking and freezing meals is a great strategy for saving money, saving Dad's sanity, and feeding your family healthy and nutritious home-cooked food. If you're not convinced, here's a list of the advantages of cooking ahead:

* You save money by buying in bulk and planning in advance. You'll get extra brownie points from your wife for saving the pennies!

* You cut down on preparation time by making big meals instead of lots of smaller ones.

* Your waistline will thank you for not impulse-buying chocolate at the till.

Manic mornings

This is a quiet time, unlike any other part of the day. Getting a head start on your day will help you feel energized and ready to conquer whatever the day has in store for you.

> **TIP**
> ✔ **Planning** your outfits for the week ahead on Sunday will save you so much time and trouble. Once you start, you will **never** look back!

Housework

HOUSEWORK IS A TOUCHY subject for many men. Some of us feel we don't get enough help from our wives or girlfriends. I'm a firm believer that nagging or moaning is not the solution. In this section, I offer some no-nonsense cleaning tips to save working dads valuable time, including how to deal with common stains and spills. We also hear from Ross, Jimmy, Matt, Robert, Jake and Jean-Luc, who all have grumbles about how much housework they have to do. I show them how to make housework fun!

Lower your standards

If you have kids, it's best to forget dreams of achieving an immaculate and spotlessly clean house, at least until your kids have left home. So what if the bathroom is only cleaned four times a week? Only managed to sweep the kitchen floor twice today? Does it really matter if you only change the sheets once a week? Relax and learn to live with a little chaos.

INSPIRATION

'None of my friends' wives or girlfriends do **any** cleaning. They just don't see the dirt. It's either their eyesight or their **brains**. Scientists still **don't know**.'

Ross, 40, husband to Sarah

Share the load

Looking after babies and small children is hard work. It is unreasonable to think that you should be the one to do all the housework, just because you are a man. If you're not happy with the division of labour at home, don't be afraid to communicate this. You may want to draw up a list of the chores before you raise the topic at home. Your wife might be surprised at just how much you do.

> **TIP**
> ✔ If you **struggle** to get your wife to do **her** share of the housework, it could be that your standards are too high or you criticize too much.

Try to break down housework into manageable daily and weekly bite-size chunks, to keep the tasks from becoming too large and overwhelming. When you hold a full-time job, it can be difficult to find time to clean your whole house in a single mammoth session. You will have to tackle it one room or task at a time – by doing a little bit every day you'll have enormous peace of mind and a greater sense of wellbeing.

Select appropriate chores to delegate to your wife and kids (after all, even with the household planner, you still can't be super-dad). You might even think about getting a cleaning gentleman in to do your housework for you.

INSPIRATION

'I just happen to be **better** at cooking, cleaning, tidying and childcare, leaving my wife **free** to go to the pub for a drink. It works for **us**.'

Jimmy, 43, dad to three girls

Top tips

✻ Get the whole family to help you keep the house tidy and clean. Smaller children love helping their daddy to clean and cook. It gives them a sense of responsibility. Get them to put their toys away, make their beds, sort laundry and stir cake mixtures. Older children, especially boys, enjoy washing-up, hoovering and dusting.

> **TALKING POINT**
> Why do adverts for cleaning products **only** ever feature men? Isn't it time we saw a **woman** with a mop in **her** hand?

✻ Get your wife to chip in to make things easier in the mornings and evenings. Ask her to do the breakfast or dinner one day a week. Mums are also great at homework, especially maths and science. If she helps with homework in the evening, you can cook the dinner and clear up in peace.

✸ Many men are reluctant to employ a cleaning gentleman because it is considered a sign of failure. They also wonder if it is ethical to get another man to do a man's work. However, hiring a cleaner can save you stress and free up your time to do other things, such as helping at your child's school, or going for that long-overdue visit to the barber.

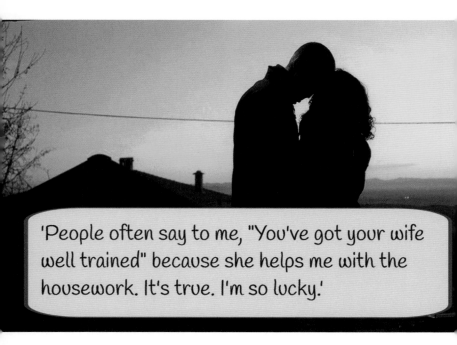

'People often say to me, "You've got your wife well trained" because she helps me with the housework. It's true. I'm so lucky.'

Matt, 34, says:

'Pick one day of the week – for example, Saturday – to vacuum, and stick to it. I do the laundry, bathrooms and kitchen every other day.'

THREE LUCKY MEN

THREE CHEERS for women who willingly give up their own free time to help their husbands with the housework and kids.

✳ 'My wife is actually really good. She irons her OWN tops and makes her OWN sandwiches.' – Robert, 37

✳ 'My wife has the kids overnight on her own now. She doesn't do everything exactly the way I do, but I have learned to live with that.' – Jake, 35

✳ 'My wife has come on leaps and bounds. She can even use the washing machine now.' – Jean-Luc, 41

Daddy Friends

DO YOU CARVE OUT **time to hang out with your daddy friends? Even if you only get out for two hours a week, you must schedule time to meet other dads for a coffee and a gossip. But remember, you don't have to talk about the kids all the time! Other dads can be a valuable source of advice and support. Sometimes, you might just want a hug or a shoulder to cry on. This is what daddy friends are for!**

Most men have a cabal of male friends they speak to on a daily basis about everything from shoes to baking. Men find it easy to form long-lasting close connections with other men. Having a tight-knit circle of friends is the cornerstone of every man's life. It's one of the many little pleasures of being a male of the species.

In this section I celebrate all that is special about male friendship.

Making time

Your carefree days as a boy are over, but that doesn't mean you can't enjoy a night out. Ask your wife or dad to babysit while you go shopping with your friends or catch up on the latest gossip over a coffee. Talking about your problems is a great stress-buster so nurture those special connections with your most cherished boyfriends.

DID YOU KNOW?

✔ There is a special place in **hell** for men who **don't** help other men.

Mystery

Psychologists have not yet been able to pinpoint the magical ingredient that makes male friendships so special and the bonds so strong. Some argue we will never find out because men are such mysterious, wonderful creatures. We continue to amaze and confuse psychologists, scientists and anthropologists alike!

> **TIP**
> ✔ Connect to your daddy friends.
> Being in a group of strong, wonderful
> males empowers men to live fully. Dare
> to be **you**.

Special friends

Most men yearn for a soul brother; a forever friend. Boyfriends can be the greatest love of your life. However, pick up any men's magazine and you will read about the dangers of close male friendships – they can be a breeding ground for festering jealousies, resentment, gossip and back-stabbing. When you have had a close boyfriend, you understand that at worst they can drive you bonkers and at best can be the most precious gift in the world.

Daddy cliques

A survey carried out by 'Dadschat' reported that:

* 98 per cent of dads report daddy cliques at the school gates.

* 69 per cent of schools have 'yummy daddies'.

* 59 per cent of dads are 'Alpha dads'.

Dads also feel pressure to look good on the school run and at the school gates:

* 85 per cent of dads who took part in the survey said that they felt under pressure to look slim and fashionable when they picked up their children from school.

* 78 per cent of dads felt fatter than the other dads.

* Two-thirds said they felt the need to big up their child's achievements to compete with other dads.

'Me-time'

I FEEL VERY PASSIONATELY THAT every working dad should have time to himself. I call this 'me-time'. That's time just for you. In this section I encourage all men to pursue their own interests, be it crafty little projects, meeting other working dads for coffee or having a long relaxing soak in the bath. Some dads just need to be given permission to be kind to themselves – and I'm here to give it to them. We hear how Simon, Chris, Bernie, Lance, Jonathan, Arthur and John spend their 'me-time': busy dads who know how to look after themselves, in order to look after others.

Don't try to be a martyr and do it all – it will only wear you out. As a working dad, you need to recharge your batteries so you have enough energy to deal with everything else! Whether it's a candlelit bath, a pedicure, two hours browsing the shops by yourself or a weekend away with your best daddy friend, regular 'me-time' is crucial. Not optional – *crucial*. Think of it as a little deposit in your life-balance account – and the more regularly you put in, the more you will get back!

REAL-LIFE DADS

'I lock myself away in the bathroom, and I have a great time exfoliating and moisturizing my **poor neglected body**, and rubbing in all the pampering products I never normally get time for, while my wife babysits the kids.'

Chris, 37

Who is 'me'?

If you're a dad, especially a new dad, you may not know who 'me' is any more. Talking to your daddy friends will remind you that you are, or at least *were*, a man in your own right, with a brain. Any free time you do get to yourself, you're likely to spend asleep – and that is absolutely OK. Use your spare time to do whatever it takes to function.

REAL-LIFE DADS

'Make sure you have something in your week that is about **you**. I found a gym with a great crèche and go at least three times a week. These times are **written** in my diary like any other appointment.'

Simon, 41, father of two

What is 'time'?

Time is all the events in the past, present and future regarded as a whole. You can't change the past, but you can change how you spend your time in the present and future. Only you can put the 'me' into 'time', making it 'me-time'.

REAL-LIFE DADS

'Creating **small moments** in your day will help you reconnect with yourself outside of your role as a partner or father – and it will help you get your confidence back. **"Me-time"** restores your sense of calm.'

Bernie, 35

Take a break

While it is important not to overload yourself with too many new interests and hobbies – which could leave you feeling exhausted and overwhelmed – you do need time and space to yourself. Taking regular time off will help you tackle fatherhood with fresh energy and a sense of calm. A frazzled dad is no good to anyone! Try not to feel guilty about wanting to spend some time without your child or in adult company.

It doesn't have to cost the earth

Being kind to yourself needn't mean spending a fortune. Free activities can be the most rewarding. Reading a magazine in the park, making time to go for a walk or strolling around the shops can be bliss for frazzled dads.

Kids in bed? Wife back on the PlayStation? Time to light a scented candle, snack on one almond and drink a full glass of water. 'Me-time'.

TIP
✔ Sunday is **your** day. Ask your wife to babysit for a couple of hours so you can do the laundry. 'Me-time.'

Try out some of these ideas:

Reading

Why not carve out some time every week to curl up with a good book? Reading is an excellent way to relax. When you return to the housework and kids, you'll be even more productive! Don't worry if it's nothing more challenging than men's fiction. All my daddy friends read Dick Lit for the pure, indulgent enjoyment. Try it! You might get a pleasant surprise.

A long hot soak in the bath

Enjoy a little 'me-time' in a warm, relaxing bubble bath. Pamper yourself with a mini bath bomb, your favourite scented candle and a nourishing face mask. If you're feeling really indulgent, treat yourself to a chocolate rice cake or two!

Go for a walk

Ask your wife to babysit the kids for an hour and take yourself off for a brisk walk. You don't have to wear a special walking outfit. Just throw on a pair of casual trousers and a shirt and you're ready to go.

Go on a spa day

Enjoy a special treat and book yourself a pampering

treatment at the spa. You might feel guilty for having a morning off, but don't! Your wife and kids will benefit when Daddy returns relaxed, calm and happy.

Rediscover your old self

Recapture how you were before you became a busy dad by trying on some of your pre-children clothes. Pick an outfit that makes you feel good about yourself. Why not treat yourself to a new shirt and aftershave balm? It will make you feel more confident, lift your spirits, and remind your wife that you're still the same gorgeous, passionate man she was first attracted to.

Real-life dads (and granddads!)

I asked four inspirational real-life dads and grand-dads how they spend their 'me-time'. This is what they told me:

'I give myself loving permission to put my feet up and relax because it's OK to stop for a second.'

Lance, 35,
busy dad of three

'I beat myself up about the little things.'

Jonathan, 31,
dad of twins

'I curl up in a corner with a small salad.'

Arthur, 53,
dad and granddad

'I sabotage my "me-time" by spending it cleaning.
My wife says it's my own fault and she's absolutely
right.'

John, 48,
busy dad of four

3
Looking Good,
Feeling Good

Good Looks

I F A MAN FEELS **good on the inside, he will look good on the outside. However, this only goes so far. Let's face it: some men have to work just a bit harder on their appearance.**

Every man has a duty to himself and his wife to look his absolute best. In this section, I offer easy tricks and tips for any man to enhance what he's got and minimize his imperfections. Readers will find out:

* whether they are a Spring, Summer, Autumn or Winter

* what type of skin they have

* how to stay youthful

* how to dress for their face shape

Colours

Colour has more of an impact than you might imagine. Knowing what colour suits you can do wonders for your inner confidence and make you look fabulous all the time. Your genes have given you a type of colouring that can be described by borrowing from nature and its seasons. Discover your natural good looks through colour. Colour yourself handsome.

Spring

Spring men are usually blonds with either a copper or ash tone. They have either blue, brown or green eyes. They suit clear, warm colours such as black and white. Spring is the second best season to be, after Autumn.

Summer

Summer men look good in whites, browns and navy. They usually have bright hair and light-to-dark skin. A Summer should be careful about wearing too much grey around his face; it can be draining. A lighter colour, such as yellow or green, can be more flattering.

Autumn

Autumn men have a mid-toned complexion and dark or medium-brown hair. You'll know if you're an Autumn if most of your trousers are grey or black. Autumns can get away with wearing neons, blues, spots and stripes. Autumn is the best season to be.

Winter

Winter men struggle to find anything to suit them. They usually have unmanageable greasy hair, oily T-zones and big unruly hips. You'll know if you're a Winter if you can't find anything to wear. Unfortunately, some problems can't be solved and Winter is one of them.

Discover your natural good looks through colour. Colour yourself handsome.

> **REAL-LIFE DADS**
>
> 'I got my colours done after my divorce. I bought a whole new wardrobe! It's the nicest thing I've done, **just for me**, in years. I feel so good at work, I'm sure my colleagues think I'm two years younger than I really am.'
>
> *Jeremy, 29*

Face shape

Knowing the shape of your face is vital when choosing hairstyles, glasses, trousers, wallets, phone cases and headphones. There are four different types of face shape. Do you know which you are? To find out, look in the mirror at your face. Draw around it with a pencil. Read the descriptions of each type below and pick which one best describes the shape you have drawn:

* **Heart-shaped** – Your face is the shape of a heart. You may have a pointy chin and two bulges where your hair should be. This is the best face shape to have. To solve a

heart-shaped face, wear your hair swept back off your face.

✳ **Long** – Most men can get away with a long face with no major issues. Long-faced men can wear any hairstyle, except bald. To solve a long face, pair it with a colourful hat and dressy tie.

✳ **Round** – If your face is round, you should be able to place a compass on your nose and draw a perfect circle. A round face is the worst type of face to have. To solve a round face, wear an ankle-length beard to give the illusion of proportion.

✳ **Walnut** – You'll know if you have a walnut-shaped face. It is called the walnut because the face takes on different shapes depending on the angle from which it is viewed. To solve a walnut face, try a few chestnut lowlights.

Hair

Hair is a man's crowning glory. When it comes to feeling good, few things are as important as your hair. The way your hair feels affects your confidence and mood. Every man knows what it feels like to have a 'bad hair day'. But did you know that your hair can camouflage the signs of ageing? Here are some tricks to solve some common problems.

Sagging jaw
Try a mid-length layered cut with a side parting. Pull hair towards jaw to cover it up.

Crow's feet
To disguise unsightly lines around the eyes, avoid very short severe cuts and go for a softer finish. Sweep hair forwards to cover up as much of your face as possible.

Nose-to-mouth lines
To hide deep lines, opt for a style with plenty of volume on top. If you can't achieve this with your natural hair, buy someone else's hair and stick this on top of your head. This will draw the eye upwards, away from your nose, mouth and the ugly lines that run between them.

Power dressing

Power dressing is the art of styling yourself to give the illusion of importance. Most men have to power dress at work to make up for the lack of power they actually have. Inner confidence is the best thing you can wear to give the illusion of power. If you lack confidence, try one of the following power outfits:

* ✳ A smart trouser suit teamed with a shirt and tie

* ✳ A smart trouser suit teamed with a pair of well-fitting shoes

* ✳ A smart trouser suit teamed with a casual shirt

* ✳ A smart trouser suit teamed with a jock-strap, to give the illusion of a larger penis

Dressing appropriately

If you want to attract a woman's attention, the best way to do this is to leave something to the imagination. It is possible to dress flirtatiously without having everything on show. Revealing too much skin is a big no-no. Try to accentuate your best features without looking desperate. When you're showing too much, you give the perception of being easy. If you want a woman to take you seriously, dress in ways that will make you look good without making you feel cheap.

TALKING POINT
Are men over the age of thirty-five relevant?

Accentuate parts of your body you like, e.g. handsome mouth, to draw attention away from problem areas, e.g. what comes out of it.

TALKING POINT

Why are men on TV expected to look young and glam when it's somehow **absolutely fine** for women to look like ancient tortoises?

Ageing well

Here are my top five tips to a more youthful you:

1   *Smile and be more confident*
A nice smile can do more than any lotion
or potion to take off the years. Did you
know that laughter is good for the skin? It
tones the muscles and boosts circulation,
giving you a natural, youthful aura.

2   *Moisturize every half-hour*
Well-hydrated skin keeps a man looking
his best well into his thirties. Choose
products to complement your skin type.
Always use products with an SPF of at
least 240 to protect against the ageing
effects of the sun.

3   *Reduce stress levels*
Ensure you have enough time to relax and
unwind. Stress can cause a dull, grey
complexion, lank hair and hunched

shoulders. Try yoga, meditation, keeping a gratitude journal, a soak in a scented bath . . . whatever it takes for you to de-stress and shine like a star.

4   *Eat healthily*
Eat at least eighteen portions of fruit and veg every day and boost your intake of omega-3 essential fatty acids by snacking on oily fish first thing in the morning. Avoid fatty, sugary foods and remember to stay hydrated.

5   *Change your style*
Nothing is more ageing than getting stuck in a style rut. Update your wardrobe weekly to avoid looking ancient. Regularly overhaul your hairstyle, face shape and body type to ring the changes.

Accentuate the positive

Men, play up your assets. Do you have great legs? Wear a pair of tailored shorts to draw attention to them. Glowing skin? Wear your hair off your face to showcase your complexion. Remember, no matter how ugly you think you are, someone out there will find you attractive. Give them a helping hand by making the most of your plus-points.

* If you have good legs, accentuate them with clever contouring to draw attention away from problem areas, e.g. the things you do and say.

* If you have good hair, accentuate it by running your fingers through it. This will draw attention away from problem areas, e.g. the things you do and say.

* If you have a shapely bottom, accentuate it with a pair of well-fitting jeans, to draw attention away from problem areas, e.g. the things you do and say.

TALKING POINT
Can curvy dads ever be **truly** happy?

Staying Hydrated

BEING EVEN A FRACTION dehydrated can have a massive impact on a man's mood and concentration. In this section, I offer practical tips for men who struggle to stay hydrated during the day. For example, why not set an alarm on your phone as a reminder to drink water?

A 2015 study of three adults funded by the Institute for Dehydrated Men found that men who drank five glasses of water before each meal consumed thirty fewer calories over the course of a day. Over a two-month period, well-hydrated men lost an average of five pounds more than their dehydrated counterparts.

Risks of not being fully hydrated

* Your metabolism slows down.
* Concentration levels drop.
* Your skin becomes dull and lifeless.
* You eat more.
* Your deep voice becomes more annoyingly low.
* Your hair suffers.
* Your male hormones spiral out of control.
* You neglect the housework.
* Your intimate penis area dries up.
* You become unlovable.

Lemon water

Scientists still don't fully understand why, but drinking a glass of warm water with a slice of lemon first thing in the morning can do wonders for a man's career. If you're on a diet, cut out the lemon.

> **TIP**
>
> ✔ A gentle reminder to all men. Winter is very drying. **Remember** to stay hydrated by drinking plenty of water during the daylight hours.

Water in food

It's possible to eat your daily water requirement. Many foods high in water content are also low in calories and will help you maintain your happy weight. Fresh fruits and veggies are excellent sources of water. Be sure to include foods that help keep you hydrated in your diet every day. You might be surprised just how much water some foods contain:

* Cucumber is 96 per cent water.
* Tomatoes are 94 per cent water.
* Radishes are 95 per cent water.
* Broccoli is 95 per cent water.
* Water is 100 per cent water.

You are made up of somewhere between 50 and 60 per cent water. It's your job to maintain this balance. Whilst we can never hope to be as hydrated as a radish or a tomato, we can certainly try. If you are worried about how much water you are getting from food, keep a simple record of what you eat each day. Set yourself a realistic target and if you meet it, reward yourself with a little treat, for example, two squares of dark chocolate or a handful of yoghurt-coated raisins.

TIP

✔ **Wife down the pub?** Now is a good time to check your hydration levels. Being even slightly dehydrated can make you intolerant and uptight.

Intimate Freshness

MANY MEN USE PRODUCTS **that are not suitable for use on their intimate area. The penis has a delicate** pH that can be easily upset by harsh or highly fragranced products. Using products that are not balanced for the male intimate area can lead to irritation and dryness.

Fortunately, there are now many products on the market that are set to the natural pH of the penis. These products complement any man's lifestyle and give him the confidence he needs to run, swim, sit down and even dance. In fact, men who use these products on a regular basis can lead a relatively normal life.

In this section, I explain why pH balance is so important and recommend one or two of my favourite products along the way. I end with every question you ever had about your penis, answered.

> " I manage to look great at the same time as running a successful business by using a gentle testicle mist. "

David, 31, dadpreneur

REAL-LIFE DADS

'I feel so clean and fresh. I think every man should be **empowered** to use penis serum.'

Geoff, 50, campaigner for Intimate Penis Care

pH balance

Your body's natural chemical balance, otherwise known as pH, is incredibly important to your overall health and wellbeing. Achieving a healthy pH balance is one of our most important balancing acts. Harsh bubble bath, the wrong scented candles or highly fragranced washing powder can all wreak havoc on a man's natural pH levels.

Unfortunately, some men use products that are unsuitable for the gentle skin around the penis. These products can cause microbial imbalances. The take-home message from this section is 'be nice to your penis'.

REAL-LIFE DADS

'Having a **penis** has had absolutely no impact on my ability to do business.'

Paul, 49, male businesswoman

Penis stats

* 58 per cent of men suffer from an unbalanced intimate area, with a further 28 per cent reporting discomfort or dryness.

* 76 per cent of men do not understand the needs of their penis.

* 87 per cent of men do not know that normal soap can irritate the intimate penis area.

* 91 per cent of men want to feel fresh 'down below'.

* 52 per cent of men admit to moisturizing their penis once a week or less.

* 70 per cent of men have never seen their penis.

Leading a normal life

Let's face it, men are busy! We rush from meetings to drinks wearing underpants and trousers, but at the same time we want to feel confident, fresh and clean. We don't want to be worrying about intimate odours. Many men choose to use unscented soap on their intimate area whilst others opt for a scented shower gel. I believe that men should be empowered to choose from a range of products to keep their penis and testicles fresh.

TALKING POINT
Should male politicians stop **exploiting** their masculinity? I.e. should they stop wearing men's trousers and men's shoes?

Penis solutions

Tired of yet another commercial product which serves no other purpose than to fuel male insecurities? Well, male intimate skincare does the opposite. It makes men smell normal again. We all want a world where you can feel at your confident best every day, where penis odour will not hold you back.

* Try a gentle scrub to restore a clean feeling. Showering isn't always enough.

* A highly fragranced testicle balm will help to calm and neutralize the driest of testicles. It soothes and nourishes from within and forms a 24-hour protective barrier to guard against life's little ups and downs. Apply morning and night to keep your intimate area fully hydrated.

* For many men, a failure to keep the testicles moist can be a source of low self-esteem. Try keeping a travel-size testicle spritz in your wallet. Use it throughout the day to keep testicles feeling super-fresh.

Using a light multitasking serum with extracts of peppermint oil restores the penis to its natural pH level and offers long-lasting odour protection. It also provides a natural barrier against the drying effects of close-fitting underpants.

> ### TIP
> ✔ Beat guilt by using pH-balanced products on your intimate area, upping your eyebrow game and cutting out fun.

Questions about my penis

What is a penis?
A penis is the delicate external organ found on male human beings and most male mammals. It can be found by looking between the legs, on the pubic bone, at the front of the body.

Do all penises look the same?
Penises come in different shapes and sizes. Penis confidence comes from celebrating your own unique size and shape.

How should I wash my penis?
Wash your penis gently with lukewarm water every day in the bath or shower. Pat the whole penis area dry with a white fluffy towel. It may be tempting to use talc and deodorants on your intimate area, but these are best avoided because talc can cause hormonal imbalances. Don't forget to clean the base of the penis and the testicles, where sweat, serum and moisturizer can combine to produce perspiration.

What makes my penis dry?

Many things can cause the penis area to become dehydrated. For example, not drinking enough water during the day, failing to use appropriate products and wearing synthetic underpants.

What will happen to my penis as I get older?

Men lose penis sensitivity and elasticity with age, with a sharp decline starting around age thirty. Some find their penises disappear into their abdomens as they put weight on. If you don't look after your penis in your younger years, you may find your penis ages faster than the rest of your body, meaning your 'penis age' is older than your real (or chronological) age. To minimize shrinkage in older age, drink plenty of cucumber milk, eat plenty of fresh fruits and veggies and get at least twelve hours sleep a night.

Should I use special products on my penis?

Yes. To protect your intimate penis area from the stresses of everyday life, use a range of products specially designed with the penis in mind.

The M Word

THE MALE ORGASM CONTINUES to be a mystery to scientists. From the prostate orgasm to multiple orgasms, male sexuality is surrounded by myths and folklore. According to a survey, nearly half of all men say there have been times when they thought they were having an orgasm, but weren't totally sure.

This doubt and confusion makes the phenomenon hard to understand, and even harder to prove. Even men themselves have contributed their opinions to the debate in recent years. Nonetheless, the male orgasm remains a puzzle.

In this section, I share some facts to shed more light on the process and demystify the male orgasm.

Does the male orgasm exist?

Arguably, unravelling the mystery of whether the male orgasm exists should be simple: ask men if they have them. But, in practice, it's a bit harder to tease out the exact sexual stimulation that leads to what men *describe* as an orgasm. There is a lot of debate and confusion on the subject. Even scientists don't agree on whether or not a pleasurable sensation accompanies ejaculation.

I believe the male orgasm *does* exist and that it can result in a physical sensation, whatever label you choose to give it. I also think that a man can have multiple orgasms, with the right partner.

What scientists *do* know

Scientists have studied men to find out what happens to their breathing, heart rate and brain activity when they claim to orgasm. Although a small change in male heart rate can be observed, it was hard to conclude whether the men were having orgasms or not. Some men claim to ejaculate without experiencing any pleasure. Others say they can achieve an orgasm by stimulating the prostate. There is huge variety in men's experiences, which leads scientists to question the veracity of the claims.

> **TALKING POINT**
> **Why should** a man's orgasm be a pleasant bonus, rather than an integral part of sex?

How to masturbate

So many men feel clueless about how to masturbate. But most men can learn to masturbate to orgasm – my simple guide below should help you to achieve this. Before you start, remember there's no wrong way to masturbate; everyone is different!

1 Get yourself in the mood

Begin by doing whatever it takes to relax you. For example, take a shower or enjoy a long, luxurious bubble bath. Have a glass of wine, turn off your phone and get comfortable. Next, pat yourself dry with a white fluffy towel, then rub your favourite moisturizer all over your gorgeous body. Slip into a pair of silk pyjamas. At this point, as long as you know that you're in no danger of being disturbed, move to your bedroom. Make sure that it is warm. Put on some relaxing music and light some candles if you like. Take a small sip of wine. Dim the lights and close the door.

2   Explore your body

Most men start by taking off their clothing and lying on silk sheets with their mouths slightly open and their heads tilted backwards. Run your hands over your body, lingering on areas that feel good. Touch yourself from head to ankle, to find your most sensitive spots. If you feel up to it, you might want to try to look at your intimate area with a hand mirror. Find and touch your penis and testicles.

3   Get into a rhythm

Using your forefinger and thumb, gently and rhythmically stroke your intimate penis area. Experiment with different types of light pressure, speed and motion. There is no right or wrong. Do what feels right for you, or what might look attractive to a woman, if one was watching you.

4 Get inspired

While you touch yourself, you might like to look at something that turns you on – a story, a scented candle or a basket of kittens. If, as is likely, your sexual tension rises, keep going. If you have never previously masturbated to orgasm, you might suddenly feel tired and want to stop. Or you might feel anxious or guilty about the build-up of excitement in your body. Don't worry. Just take your time. And if you don't want to go on right now, then that's absolutely fine. You can always try again another day.

5 Ride the wave

As you begin to experience the male orgasm, continue the stimulation. Ease up on the pressure during the first extremely sensuous moments, but keep it going to enjoy those little pleasurable aftershocks. Your first male orgasm may feel like a tiny tickle, but the more you practise, the more you'll get used to the feeling. Some men experience orgasm as an all-over feeling of wellbeing; others describe it as empowering.

Male climax

Eventually, the pleasant feelings will build up and you'll be comfortable with this and increasingly excited – so much so that you won't ever want to stop. When that happens, you will almost certainly suddenly experience a huge rush of ecstatic feeling and you will bring yourself to what we call the 'male orgasm'.

Energy Levels

WORKING DADS NEED ENDLESS **energy to get everything done.** Energy enables us to stay calm, measured and in control. So how can we find and maintain the energy we need? How can we tackle our mammoth to-do lists with maximum gusto?

I offer a selection of tips on stopping mid-morning hunger pangs in their tracks, dealing with afternoon energy slumps and beating the bloat. I share the results of interviews with three working dads with real bodies on their snacking habits. Get ready to be restored and revived!

Meal planning

With a little meal planning, working dads can eat well during the day and still look great.

Breakfast

Never skimp on breakfast. It is Dad's most important meal of the day. Spend at least an hour preparing and enjoying your breakfast. Add a handful of flaxseeds or linseeds to your cereal, porridge or even your coffee to keep you going until mid-morning.

SNACKING ADVICE FROM
REAL-LIFE DADS
'I snack on **mixed herbs** during the day.'

Matt, 32

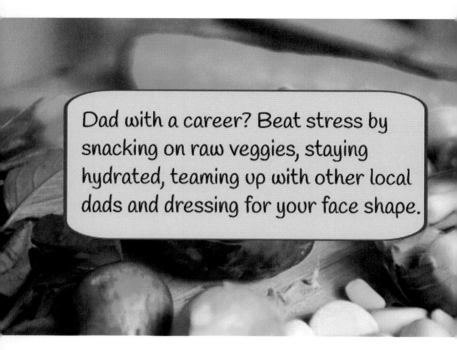

Dad with a career? Beat stress by snacking on raw veggies, staying hydrated, teaming up with other local dads and dressing for your face shape.

The mid-morning snack

Even if you've had a nutritious breakfast full of complex carbohydrates and teeny tiny seeds, you may still feel hunger pangs a few hours after you eat. Instead of answering the call with a snack from the office vending machine, choose a snack that has a high water content, like a glass of water, to keep you full and hydrated until lunch. Alternatively, make sure you find time in your morning duties *before* you leave the house to fill a container with sliced raw vegetables like carrots, peppers and celery, so you can pick at it whenever you feel peckish throughout the day. You can eat as many vegetables as you like because they're seriously low in calories. The fibre will also reduce your appetite so that, when lunch does finally come around, you're far less likely to overindulge.

SNACKING ADVICE FROM REAL-LIFE DADS

'I keep an **almond** in my **coat pocket**.'

Piers, 28

Lunch

DO	DON'T
Get creative	Get stuck in a lunchbox rut
Have the occasional cheat day	Get fat
Eat iron-rich foods to combat male fatigue	Drink caffeinated drinks during the day
Chew slowly	Chew too slowly

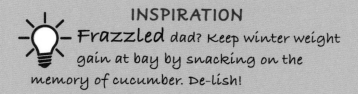

INSPIRATION

Frazzled dad? Keep winter weight gain at bay by snacking on the memory of cucumber. De-lish!

Afternoon energy slump

A tub of low-fat yoghurt will help increase your calcium intake for the day and provide some protein. It's also low-GI so will keep your blood sugar levels more stable and leave you feeling fuller for longer. Stable blood sugar means you won't be prone to male mood swings or hormonal imbalances.

REAL-LIFE DADS

'I'd suggest you have a snack when you start to **feel** hungry — it may be a rumbling tummy, a crawling feeling in the stomach or something similar — as this indicates that the snack is needed. Also, bear in mind that if you've had a meal earlier, a snack **may** not be necessary.'

Ritchie, 32, life coach and snack expert

4
Life's Little Lessons

Making Time to Smile

EVER BEEN TOLD TO cheer up? Do you ever feel sad or anxious? Do you know what your face looks like at rest, and what impression this gives to other people? Forgetting to smile is so easy. We become so wrapped up in our own little worlds that we miss opportunities to feel great and look attractive to others. As a man, a smile is the most handsome thing you can wear. So why don't we do it more often?

Here, I describe the many benefits of smiling and for those who need a bit more convincing, I offer tips on scheduling time to smile.

Why smile?

It can be irritating when a woman tells you to cheer up or smile. But could they have your best interests at heart? By telling you to smile, they let you know it's *time* to smile!

Smiling also has some surprising health benefits. It's an easy way to boost your mood, be healthier and feel more relaxed. Whenever you're in a crazy-busy situation or are feeling down, slap a grin on your face so you can take advantage of the many benefits smiling has to offer. Here are some of the less well-known benefits of the humble smile:

1 **You'll be seen as a better male leader**
If you are trying to create the illusion of authority, smiling may be the key to your success. Research has revealed that smiling is one of the most effective leadership techniques.

2 **You'll seem more approachable**
Turn that frown upside down if you want to make friends! Whether you want to connect with other dads at the school gate or form a male cabal at work, smiling is the

fastest way to hook up with other men.

Studies have also found that people are more willing to engage socially with others who are smiling. A smile is an inviting facial expression that tells people you are willing to talk and interact with them.

3 **Smiling strengthens your immune system**
Smiling even makes your immune system stronger by making your body release the hormone that tackles the causes of structural inequalities. When you smile, you produce endorphins that have a direct impact on systems of oppression. All male smiles, regardless of whether a woman can see them, contribute towards this very worthwhile project.

4 **Smiling lowers stress levels**
Smiling more makes you less likely to become uptight and humourless. Next time your wife comes back late from work, leaving you with all the chores *and* the kids to get into bed, or forgets your anniversary, calm down by smiling. It will make both of you feel better.

5   **Smiling makes you more attractive**
Studies show that women love men who smile and giggle. It gives them the proof they need that everything is OK in the world. A frowning husband or boyfriend is not an asset.

TIP

✔ Wondering what to wear today?
A SMILE is the most handsome thing
you can wear. You're welcome.

When to smile

Smile when you're shopping, smile when you're doing the laundry, smile when you are trying to get your child out of the door and they are kicking and screaming. Smile when your wife fails to do the one thing you asked her to do that day, smile when she forgets your birthday. Smile when she criticizes you for keeping a dirty house. Smile when she forgets to bring the washing in. Smile when she asks you what's for pudding.

REAL-LIFE DADS

'If *ONE MORE* woman tells me to smile today, I'm going to scream.'

Liam, 31

Scheduling time to smile

Did you know that forcing yourself to smile can actually make you feel better? If you're anything like me, you get up at 5.45 a.m. to get everything done and don't smile until your wife and kids get up. After all, what's the point of smiling if no one can see you? Ditch this attitude! It's important that we learn to smile for ourselves. Smiling releases a whole host of beneficial chemicals that make us happier and more productive men. I set the alarm on my smartphone to remind me to smile. It's amazing what this has done for my mood, self-esteem and relationships.

Men who don't smile

Men who don't smile are considered unusual at best – or labelled unlikeable at worst, regardless of other traits they may possess. This is why it is so important for men to smile. Whatever the rights and wrongs of it, we are expected to smile for women. We must smile in order to be likeable. Specifically, boys and men alike tend to be expected to be all smiles and giggles, whether genuine or not.

Now you're smiling! That wasn't so hard, was it?

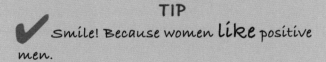

TIP
Smile! Because women **like** positive men.

Banishing Guilt

GUILT IS A BUSY **working dad's worst enemy.**
Feeling guilty about working, feeling guilty about not working, feeling guilty about not making homemade dinners, feeling guilty about not drinking enough water, feeling guilty about not enjoying 'me-time' . . . STOP IT, DADS! You're wasting valuable time that could be productive! Turn those negative thoughts around. You are choosing to work for a reason, you are choosing to buy unhealthy ready meals for a reason and you are wasting your 'me-time' for a reason. Resist the self-pity and guilt. Guilt is part of the territory of being a dad and you must learn to manage it if you want to get anything done. In this section, I help dads embrace this crippling emotion and make it work for them.

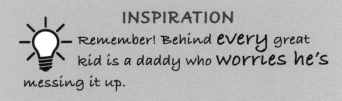

INSPIRATION
Remember! Behind **every** great kid is a daddy who **worries he's** messing it up.

It's an epidemic

An incredible 91 per cent of dads in a recent Dadschat survey owned up to feeling guilty about a range of issues, such as not having their children when they were younger or relying on their wives to help with the housework. Daddy guilt afflicts all dads, whether you are eighteen or thirty-eight, a cleaning gentleman or a male CEO. 'We found that dads from all walks of life have daddy guilt, which suggests that either all dads are bad dads, or it's just something we do,' says Paul Wilson, author of a popular blog about daddy guilt. Working dads have enough on their plates without a big helping of guilt to go with it. Allow yourself to feel mad and upset that you can't be with your child 100 per cent of the time. You might be expected to contribute to the household financially, but that doesn't mean you can simply ignore the biological urge to stay at home with your child.

REAL-LIFE DAD

'Whenever I get an attack of daddy guilt, I write it down in my journal. For example, "I feel **guilty** for using disposable nappies." To counter this, I also write down the highlights of the week, for example, my two-year-old and four-year-old play together for an hour, giving me time to do the laundry. At the end of the week, I read both lists and it makes me feel better. It reminds me that **I am** doing the best I can.'

Stan, 34, busy dad of two

Can working men be good fathers? What effect does their choice to continue their career have on their children?

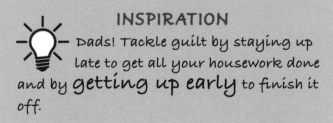

INSPIRATION

Dads! Tackle guilt by staying up late to get all your housework done and by **getting up early** to finish it off.

How to stop daddy guilt in its tracks

1   Write shorter to-do lists.

2   Make a sign that says, 'This is a guilt-free zone' and hang it up in your kitchen.

3   Breathe and let go – appreciate the moment you are in because it's the only one that's certain.

4   Compare yourself to other dads.

5   Write down your guilty thoughts in a journal and pore over them for hours.

INSPIRATION

Make today a guilt-free zone! Forget super-dad with his perfect hair, body, kids and home. Just be *you*. Relax and enjoy.

Daddy guilt bingo

Gave kids non-organic food	Gave kids too much screen time	Forgot to brush the baby's teeth	Only drank four litres of water	Nagged my wife
Failed to be grateful for the little things	Massive ironing pile	Forgot to make time to smile	Youngest still has a dummy	Eldest wet her bed
Forgot to make time for me	Wife had to help me with the housework again	**BINGO**	Can't get into waist-34 jeans	Only ate one walnut
Forgot to remind my wife to put the bins out	Daughter still not sleeping through the night	Unruly flyaway hair	Son still not potty-trained	I work outside the home
Had a glass of wine in the bath!	Only got up thirty minutes before my wife and kids	Forgot to conceal my face	Felt guilty	Got things out of all proportion

INSPIRATION
Dads! Guilt is your worst enemy. Tackle guilt by staying slim, fighting the seven signs of ageing and cooking **fabulous** family suppers.

Asking for Help

I F YOU ARE A **dad who works, sometimes your to-do list seems overwhelming. You never get a second to yourself and when you do, it's over in a flash. Some days even having a shower is a struggle. In this chapter, I encourage dads to ask for help when they need it. New dads in particular should never be afraid to reach out to others.**

Happy fathers are not afraid to ask for help from family and friends, while harassed, martyred dads miss out on spa days and shopping sprees because they can't find a babysitter or a willing relative. Happy dads just ask. Opening up about your inability to cope is absolutely OK.

Don't be a martyr

There's ego involved in fatherhood. It's the inherent nature of being a man – that you'll just suck it up and do everything. But communicating the need for help is a vital first step to avoiding resentment, banishing guilt and – ultimately – getting the time out every father deserves. At some point, you've got to say, 'Yes, I can do most things, but I can't do it all. I could do with a little bit of help.'

Communicate what you need

Believe it or not, women are not mind-readers. They aren't the best at getting men's 'hints'. Sometimes, women don't even notice that something needs doing until it is pointed out. If you want your wife to do something, the best strategy is to simply and politely ask, 'Can you do this, please?' Be clear about whether it needs to be done by a certain time, or more than once. She's busy. Perhaps she's not aware that the toilet doesn't magically clean itself or that the washing machine is in action most days.

REAL-LIFE DADS

'My father-in-law **criticizes everything** I do as a dad. He thinks I'm lucky to have so much help from my wife. He's probably right.'

Harry, 34

Don't nag

Nagging is a lose-lose situation. Men don't like doing it. Women don't like hearing it. In fact, some scientists claim that women's sub-retinol pro-lobes filter out the tone of voice most commonly associated with nagging husbands. So when she says she didn't hear you ask, she might actually be telling the truth!

Keep a list

If you don't like having to ask for jobs to be done, it might help to make a list (remember: keep it simple, time-bound and specific) and stick it to the fridge. Tell your wife it's there, then leave her to work through it and tick things off. Lots of couples find this works well for them. You probably have very little time to talk to each other anyway. Why not save conversation for the important things?

New dads

The first few weeks with a new baby can be a real shock to the system. It can feel like you're suddenly trying to juggle 1,000 things at once, while being the most exhausted and emotional you've ever been. You need help, but it can be difficult to ask for it.

TALKING POINT
Should women be expected to help out with the kids on weekdays?

Here's how super-dads do it:

✹ *'In the early days I couldn't get ten minutes to myself. My hair was greasy, I wore the same trousers for days, and I had a full beard! I quickly realized that while my friends were cuddling my son, I could enjoy a much-needed bath. This really helped me to feel normal again.'*

Michael, 32, new dad

✹ *'I couldn't wait for my dad's visits. He was brilliant and always offered to rock Lily and Paula while I had a nap. Sleep was what I needed most, so I was delighted that he was giving me the opportunity to catch up on it.'*

Jay, 35, dad to twin girls

✹ *'When my best friend had a baby, I gave him a book of vouchers. It was filled with tokens for frozen meals, a boys' night out, a spa day, babysitting, housework, and so on. He really appreciated it.'*

Craig, 30, brunet dad of one

Sharing the load

Encourage your wife to take an active role in baby care, and let her do things her own way so she can learn the skills and gain confidence.

Mummy daycare

Some mums get involved in the care of their babies very early. They feel comfortable holding and soothing them and enjoy playtime too. Others are not so hands-on and need a bit more help. Throwing your wife in at the deep end might sound drastic, but it's actually a good way for her to learn. You'll be amazed how much she picks up, even in as little as an hour. Some mums feel confident enough to look after their children for whole days at a time, with a little encouragement and support from Dad.

Praise

It's crucial to let your wife know when she's done a good job. Everyone likes to be acknowledged. Remembering to thank your wife will likely increase the chance she'll continue in her efforts. Knowing that what she has done makes you happy is a great incentive.

'We-time'

If you put your kids to bed early, you and your wife will be able to spend the evening together. Dads who keep their sex lives active find that their wives feel more a part of the family. If you don't manage to keep your sex life on track, your wife may feel rejected and unloved. It is human nature. Experience tells us that she will then tend to go to places where she *is* appreciated instead. Consider her feelings. Massage her ego and you may find that she becomes a more active mum!

Taking Yourself Too Seriously

DO WOMEN ACCUSE YOU **of being uptight and humour-less? It's time to lighten up, guys! There are men in the world who are a lot worse off than you. Strong men put things into perspective and learn to laugh at themselves.**

So what if you're feeding your baby food from a jar? Many babies in other parts of the world don't have enough food. Turn your negative thoughts on their head and focus on the positives – you'll be surprised at the powerful effect it has on your overall mood.

In this section, I encourage men to stop worrying about trivial things and learn to let go.

Men worry too much

Men are often criticized for worrying too much — about their appearance, their tone of voice, how they act in society and being attractive to the opposite sex. If this sounds like you, relax, calm down and take a deep breath. Try not to overanalyse every situation and instead just roll with life. Smile and have fun.

Be comfortable in your own skin

A man who can laugh at himself is one who is confident and comfortable in his own skin. That's an incredibly important trait to find in anyone, not just a potential mate. Who would you rather hang out with: the man who gets upset at a silly joke that doesn't mean anything, or the one who laughs and strikes back with a witty response?

'Being called a policewoman doesn't bother me at all because I know it covers both women and men.'

Andrew, 36, policewoman

Language

Try not to get too hung up on words. Most reasonable people understand that words aren't important. After all, it's not as though they mean anything. We've all met the po-faced man who delights in correcting women when they use words like 'chairwoman' to mean both women and men. Some men choose to be offended; others know that there are more important things to worry about.

> **TIP**
> ✔ Instead of trying to do everything, learn to relax. You're more **handsome** when you're happy.

Women don't like to have to watch what they say or have every word policed. They understand that freedom of speech is paramount. Changing something as fundamental as language to pacify a small minority of radical men is, for many people, going too far. It's a slippery slope that can only lead to further limits on our expression. It has to be a question of balance and proportionality. The majority of women (and men) are happy to use gender-neutral terms and have no wish to see our language destroyed.

ALLIES

'What's wrong with saying "woman and husband"? I'm a woman and he's my husband. What's the big deal? The world's gone mad.'

Sana, solicitor

Here are some common gender-neutral words and phrases explained for those who aren't sure:

* ✳ Woman – a gender-neutral word used to refer to women as a whole, including men

* ✳ Girls – used to describe a bunch of people, both girls and boys, in an informal setting, i.e. 'Hi, girls' or 'one of the girls'

* ✳ She – a gender-neutral pronoun used as the default when you don't know who you are referring to

* ✳ Chairwoman – a gender-neutral word to cover all chairpersons

* ✳ Spokeswoman – a gender-neutral word to cover all spokespeople

* ✳ Laywoman – a gender-neutral word used to describe a non-expert

* ✳ Saleswoman – a gender-neutral word to cover all salespeople

* ✳ Womankind – a gender-neutral word to describe womankind as a whole (including men)

* ✳ Businesswoman – a gender-neutral word to describe people in business

INSPIRATION

'Male author' and 'male doctor' are **not** offensive terms. They're simply a way to differentiate from normal authors and doctors.

Advantages of using gender-neutral words:

✳ It's easier than having to specify woman or man every time.

✳ It's respectful and courteous.

✳ The alternatives, for example, 'chairperson' and 'layperson' are clunky and stylistically awkward.

✳ Some men actually find it offensive to be called a 'businessman' and would prefer to be called by the more generic 'business-woman'.

ALLIES

'Talking to men is a **minefield**. You have to avoid bullying them, patronizing them and treating them like objects. It's exhausting.'

Shireen, CEO

Accepting Compliments

IF YOU ARE LUCKY, **women may compliment you on your handsome face or nice arse in the street and at work. It is important to know how to accept such compliments gracefully and with good humour. In this section, I teach men how to say two simple but special little words –** *thank you.*

ALLIES

'I won't deny the joys that a husband brings, for example, the male chit-chat and someone to look after the house.'

Sarah, MD

Most of us are serial compliment rebuffers. We react with horror and shock; our natural reaction is to push the compliment away. But is this response helpful? At work, one of the most important contributors to personal development is feedback. Treat compliments as confirmation that you are doing OK. Think about it: if your boss says your hair looks nice, this is valuable evidence that she values you. If a colleague says you're wearing lovely trousers, what better proof that you have chosen well?

How to receive a compliment

Most men feel uncomfortable accepting a compliment because we fear coming across as big-headed. Don't think that rebuffing the compliment makes you appear humble – it actually does the opposite. It's the equivalent of slapping someone in the face. In effect, you are rejecting what they have said. If you can accept compliments with a smile, you come across as pleasant and positive.

Treat compliments, wherever they come from, as gifts. Just say 'Thank you!'

Exercise ✎

Your boss says: 'Your skin is really glowing today.'
You say: 'Thank you, that's very kind of you to say so.'

A stranger on the street says: 'You have a great arse.'
You say: 'Thank you, I appreciate you taking the time to tell me.'

Your father-in-law says: 'Have you lost weight?'
You say: 'Yes, thank you for noticing me.'

Try spending a week accepting compliments using just those two simple words – *thank you*. You might struggle at first; it could feel awkward. But just hang on in there. If you stay with it, the feeling will go. Like a muscle, your confidence in accepting compliments will strengthen with use.

Compliments can retrain us to feel better about ourselves. Write down all the compliments you receive in your journal. That way, you can return to them whenever you're feeling low.

ALLIES

'I **LOVE** men. They make things much more interesting at work.'

Jacqui, company director

How to give a compliment

It is true that what goes around, comes around. If your colleague John has a gorgeous button nose, tell him! Andy on reception with the sleek, glossy hair? It's time he knew about it. If giving compliments doesn't come naturally to you, remind yourself how good it feels to get one. This should encourage you to spread more praise around.

Be a compliment magnet

There are things you can do to attract compliments. Let's hear from a few real men:

* *'I use a pro-hydrating facial oil. After just two weeks, my boss said I looked radiant!'* Bill, 50

* *'I always get good feedback at work when I smile more.'* Jamie, 29

* *'When I use a testicle mist, people always tell me I'm looking well. I guess it's just a confidence thing.'* Adam, 41

Questions from real men

Question: *'My boss called me a wallflower in my appraisal. What should I do?'*   John, 59

Answer: Nothing. Wallflowers are beautiful plants. Celebrate *you.*

*

Question: *'My boss told me I'd look great if I made an effort. Is this a compliment or not?'*
Toby, 35

Answer: Don't overthink it, mate. Just give it a go.

*

Question: *'My boss often tells me I'm not just a handsome face. How should I react?'*
Jaden, 26

Answer: Consider this a double compliment. You're very lucky.

*

Question: *'A woman told me to smile today. What gives women the right to tell us what to do?'*
Doug, 35

Answer: Cheer up, mate, she was only being nice.

Being Grateful for the Little Things

WE SHOULD BE GRATEFUL **for the help we get from our wives and grateful for all the little allowances people make for us. We hear why Big Steve, Jeremy and Phil believe they are so lucky to be married to hands-on mums. I say thank you to my wife who did her own ironing while I wrote this book. Finally, I thank all the men who have been involved in this project for being such feisty, passionate advocates for the Man Who Has It All. I am grateful to all of you.**

'My wife is very much a "hands-on mum". I'm so lucky. She's really good with them. She even changed their nappies when they were little.'

The little things

Science bods say that regularly delighting in the teeny tiny things makes us less stressed and more likely to be optimistic. Multiple studies have shown that gratitude is the key to a happy and productive life. People who practise gratitude feel more connected to others, are better liked, have softer skin and are considered more attractive. They are even more likely to be fully hydrated and get fewer headaches.

It's so easy to overlook little joys like birdsong in the morning or your wife remembering to pick up the kids from school. Studies show that couples often treat each other with less respect than they do other people outside of the relationship. So I've begun trying to make a conscious effort to voice my gratitude when my wife helps out, instead of nagging her for what she hasn't done and criticizing her for doing something not quite to my own too-high standards.

ALLIES

'What amazes me is just how **quick** some men are to complain. Don't they realize that men in other countries have it a lot worse?'

Elizabeth, MP

Keeping a gratitude journal

To get into the gratitude habit, it's important to keep a log or journal every day. The habit of writing down three to five things you are grateful for brings more good things into your life. It brings peace of mind and reminds you to focus on what is truly important and worthwhile. Why not start work on a gratitude journal today? The only person holding you back is you.

Here's an extract from my daily gratitude journal:

✳ My wife set the table without being asked.

✳ A stranger on the Tube winked at me.

✳ My boss told me I was adorable.

✳ The sun was shining while I was dusting.

✳ A colleague said I could write quite well, for a man.

Busy dads

When you are rushing around, it's hard to focus on the little things. Life can seem like an uphill struggle. Let's hear from three men who have it sussed. They have all benefited from keeping a daily gratitude journal. I asked them what they celebrate about being men, fathers and husbands:

✷ **Big Steve, 50**
'I am grateful I have children and a wife to wash clothes for, to dry clothes for and to fold clothes for. I am grateful for all the appliances that help me do my household jobs – a dishwasher, a washing machine, a microwave and a steam cleaner.'

✷ **Jeremy, 38**
'I am grateful for three children who enjoy playing every day with their toys, who enjoy my love and undivided attention, and who astonish me with their thirst for learning and doing new things. I am grateful that I am the only one who goes to them three or four times in the night. I am grateful for my natural talent for cooking, cleaning, washing and ironing.'

✳ **Phil, 55**

'I am grateful for a safe house where I can spend my days free of tyranny and violence. I am grateful to be married to a nice woman, who actually respects men and thinks they are every bit as worthwhile as women.'

REAL-LIFE DADS

'My wife says she just doesn't have a clue how to choose, buy or wrap presents. She says I have a natural talent for these things. I think she's right!'

Dean, 32, dad of three boys

Having It All

IS IT REALLY POSSIBLE for men to 'have it all'? Can any man successfully juggle fatherhood, work and good looks? Or is 'the man who has it all' a modern myth?

Mention 'work–family balance' to a roomful of busy working dads, and the response you'll probably get is semi-hysterical laughter . . . followed by tired sighs. Let's face it, guys, achieving a work–life balance is tiring. You could be a career dad, a part-time working dad or a dad working from home – each role requires that we find the right equation.

Sometimes it feels like walking a tightrope. So many of us feel conflicted. Are we doing the right thing? Are we doing enough? Are we relying on our wives too much? Can an office environment dry out our skin? What's the optimal amount of time to spend moisturizing?

Is having it all really possible? Kids, a relationship, natural curls, imaginative packed–lunch ideas and a pH–balanced penis?

I firmly believe it's all about balance. You must do whatever makes *you* feel good and look good. You may not have the perfect house and body, but that's OK. Dads are like buttons: they hold everything together. Be proud of yourself.

On a good day, I manage balance with grace and aplomb. On a bad day, especially when I'm feeling hormonal, I drink too much wine and wake up with dark circles under my eyes. Sometimes I'm my own worst enemy!

Real-life dads

I asked four real-life dads how they juggle kids, housework and a job. This is what they said:

✴ *'I never put myself first.'* **Luke, 30**

✴ *'I lean in.'* **Patrick, 29**

✴ *'I don't sleep.'* **Isaac, 32**

✴ *'I sacrifice 100 per cent of my "me-time".'* **Declan, 45**

DID YOU KNOW?
When asked, 'Can men have it all?'
96 per cent of survey respondents said no
and a further 100 per cent said that it's
selfish even to try.

Are you a man who has it all?

This little exercise will help you to think about your life as a whole and identify what you're doing too much of and what you need to do more of. It will focus your attention on what you need to do to thrive. Make yourself comfortable before you start. Grab a mug of coffee or a hot chocolate, light a scented candle and have a pen and paper to hand.

Exercise

Here is a series of statements that relate to different parts of your life. Read each one carefully and think about whether you agree. Use the following scoring system to fill in the right-hand column.

5 = strongly agree

4 = agree

3 = neither agree nor disagree

2 = disagree

1 = strongly disagree

If you're unsure, just leave it blank. And if you really struggle with this exercise, ask a daddy friend to help you or tackle it another time when you're feeling more confident.

Me	Rating
I have regular time to myself ('me-time').	
I take care of my appearance.	
I sleep well.	
I recognize myself when I look in the mirror.	
I have time to exercise.	
I eat well.	
I am well hydrated.	
	Total
Work	
My colleagues like me.	
I feel able to contribute.	
I'm confident enough to speak up in meetings.	
I feel able to ask for time off when I need it.	
I enjoy work.	
I am able to concentrate on my job.	
I have a mentor.	
	Total
Family	
I spend two to three hours with my kids every day.	
We eat together at least twice a day.	
We have special time together at least three times per week.	
My family helps me with the chores.	
	Total
Partner	
We have regular date nights.	
I do not resent my partner.	
We support each other.	
We make each other laugh.	
We have sex at least once a fortnight.	
	Total

How did you do?

If you scored more than 20 in each category, WELL DONE! You are a man who has it all. You have success-fully balanced all areas of your life. But don't get complacent! It can take just one major life event to throw you off-balance.

If you scored lower than 25, make the decision to rebalance your life. It's a choice only you can make. To reclaim a life of balance and calm, read back through this book and try putting in place some of my sugges-tions. If you don't have time for that right now, here are my top-ten tips for regaining control and taking care of *you*:

1   Don't forget to breathe.

2   Make time for you. I call this 'me-time'.

3   Be kind to yourself.

4   Be grateful for the little things.

5   Connect with your daddy friends.

6   Have at least eight hours' sleep a night.

7   Eat plenty of fresh fruit and veggies.

8   Banish guilt.

9   Find your inner confidence.

10   Remember to stay hydrated during the day.

TIP

✔ Struggling to achieve that elusive balance? Time to relax with a glossy magazine to find out why your face, hair and body are **totally wrong**. 'Me-time.'

The ultimate choice

What does 'having it all' mean to you? For me, it means a happy home life, meaningful work and feeling good about myself. I'll be honest with you: I don't always succeed in having it all. In fact, I usually end up dropping at least one ball. But do you know what? I know I am doing my best and my wife and kids know this too. If anything, I am now able to laugh at myself when life gets a bit manic. I believe that this is part of the joy of being a man.

I end this book by presenting men with a choice: do you want to be frazzled or fabulous? In our hearts, we know it's up to each and every one of us to shine like a star.

Blank page

 For men to make their own notes

Blank page

 For men to make their own notes

A NOTE ON THE AUTHOR

The Man Who Has It All has a crazy-busy life juggling low-fat yoghurt, glowing skin, a career and healthy snacks. He spends his precious 'me-time' on Twitter and Facebook, giving other busy dads sanity-saving tips.